PHARRELL WILLIAMS

★ MUSIC STAR ★

KATIE LAJINESS

Big Buddy Books
An Imprint of Abdo Publishing
abdopublishing.com

BIG BUDDY POP BIOGRAPHIES Peachtree

abdopublishing.com

Published by Abdo Publishing, a division of ABDO, PO Box 398166, Minneapolis, Minnesota 55439.
Copyright © 2016 by Abdo Consulting Group, Inc. International copyrights reserved in all countries.
No part of this book may be reproduced in any form without written permission from the publisher.
Big Buddy Books™ is a trademark and logo of Abdo Publishing.

Printed in the United States of America, North Mankato, Minnesota.
102015
012016

THIS BOOK CONTAINS RECYCLED MATERIALS

Cover Photo: Brad Barket/Stringer/Getty.
Interior Photos: Associated Press (pp. 11, 17); Bryan Bedder/Getty (p. 27); James Devaney/Getty
    (p. 13); Kevork Djansezian/Getty (p. 19); Scott Gries/Getty (pp. 11, 13); Frazer Harrison/Getty
    (p. 5); Jason LaVeris/Getty (p. 25); Paul Natkin/Getty (p. 15); Johnny Nunez/Getty (p. 9);
    Joel Ryan/Invision/AP (p. 29) Matt Sayles/Invision/AP (p. 21); Richard Shotwell/Invision/AP
    (pp. 6, 23, 25).

Coordinating Series Editor: Tamara L. Britton
Contributing Editor: Marcia Zappa
Graphic Design: Jenny Christensen

Library of Congress Cataloging-in-Publication Data

Lajiness, Katie.
  Pharrell Williams / Katie Lajiness.
      pages cm. -- (Big buddy pop biographies)
  Includes index.
  ISBN 978-1-68078-063-5
1. Williams, Pharrell--Juvenile literature. 2. Singers--United States--Biography--Juvenile literature. 3.
Rap musicians--United States--Biography--Juvenile literature. I. Title.
  ML3930.W55L35 2016
  782.421649092--dc23
  [B]
                                      2015028662

CONTENTS

A BRIGHT STAR

Pharrell Williams is a gifted artist. He is a talented singer, songwriter, record **producer**, and fashion **designer**. In 2014, Pharrell became a **coach** on the television show *The Voice*.

DID YOU KNOW?

Pharrell made the first 24-hour music video. It shows different people dancing to his song "Happy." Many stars such as Jimmy Kimmell and Steve Carrell are in the video.

SNAPSHOT

NAME:
Pharrell Williams

BIRTHDAY:
April 5, 1973

BIRTHPLACE:
Virginia Beach, Virginia

POPULAR ALBUMS:
In My Mind, G I R L

MAJOR APPEARANCE:
The Voice

FAMILY TIES

Pharrell Williams was born in Virginia Beach, Virginia, on April 5, 1973. His parents are Pharoah and Carolyn Williams. His younger brothers are Cato and Psolomon.

Pharrell's family supports his work. They often attend events with him.

WHERE IN THE WORLD?

Ohio

Pennsylvania

New Jersey

Maryland

Delaware

West Virginia

Virginia

Kentucky

Virginia Beach

Tennessee

ATLANTIC OCEAN

North Carolina

SCHOOL DAYS

Pharrell attended Princess Anne High School in Virginia Beach. He has always had a lot of musical talent. Pharrell started as a drummer in the school band. In 1990, Pharrell and his friend Chad Hugo started a band called the Neptunes.

DID YOU KNOW?

Pharrell has always loved music. Growing up, he listened to music from artists such as Stevie Wonder.

Chad Hugo (*left*) and Pharrell met in the school band. Chad played the saxophone.

STARTING OUT

The Neptunes were discovered when Pharrell was still in high school. Music **producer** Teddy Riley saw them at a talent show. Soon, the Neptunes found success as music producers!

Pharrell wanted to work in the music business after high school. He worked hard to write great music for the Neptunes.

Teddy Riley taught Pharrell about the music business.

Pharrell and Chad Hugo wrote and **produced** popular songs for many singers. The Neptunes worked with Blackstreet on the *Blackstreet* album in 1994. In 2001, they produced a song with Britney Spears. "I'm a Slave 4 U" became their first worldwide hit!

In 2002, Pharrell (*second from right*) performed with well-known artists at the MTV Music Awards. They included Busta Rhymes (*left*), Diddy (*second from left*), and Usher (*right*).

Pharrell has worked with singer Kelis.

MUSICAL LIFE

In 2001, Pharrell wanted to **perform** in a new band. He started a music group called N.E.R.D. The band included Chad Hugo from the Neptunes, and their friend Shay Haley. The band **released** albums in 2002, 2004, 2008, and 2010.

Pharrell is a fan of the television show *Star Trek*. He and his N.E.R.D. bandmates, Chad (*left*) and Shay (*center*) often give a hand sign from the show.

Pharrell also wanted to write music to **perform** on his own. So in 2006, he **released** his first **solo** album, *In My Mind*. His songs are a mix of **hip-hop** and **pop** music. The album was **nominated** for a **Grammy Award**.

In 2013, Pharrell released one of his most popular songs. "Happy" was on the *Despicable Me 2* **soundtrack**. It became the number one song in 2014. That year, the song also appeared on Pharrell's second album, *G I R L*.

In My Mind reached number three on the Billboard 200 chart.

BE HAPPY!

"Happy" is about people finding what brings them joy. After the song became a hit, Pharrell teamed up with the United Nations Foundation. He worked with this group to **inspire** happiness around the world.

In 2015, Pharrell wrote a children's book inspired by the song. *Happy!* has **photographs** of happy children around the world.

Pharrell sang his song "Happy" at the 2015 Grammy Awards.

A PRODUCER'S LIFE

Pharrell has **produced** songs for many artists. He has worked with singers such as Ed Sheeran, Miley Cyrus, and Justin Timberlake.

Pharrell has won many **awards** for his great work in music. He has won ten **Grammy Awards**. He has also won seven Billboard Music Awards.

In 2013, Pharrell worked with music group Daft Punk on the song "Get Lucky." It sold more than 9 million copies.

TELEVISION STAR

In addition to his musical work, Pharrell is often on television. In 2014, he began appearing on the television show *The Voice*. As a **coach**, Pharrell helps singers get ready to **perform** on stage.

Pharrell has been a voice actor on *The Simpsons*. He has been a guest on *The Ellen DeGeneres Show* and *The Tonight Show Starring Jimmy Fallon*.

Pharrell was the winning coach on *The Voice* in 2015.

A BUSY LIFE

Pharrell likes to spend time with his family. He is married to Helen Lasichanh. They have a son named Rocket. He turned seven years old in 2015.

Pharrell creates more than music. He is also a successful clothes **designer**. Billionaire Boys Club and Icecream are his two clothes companies. He also works with shoe company Adidas to make shoes from recycled plastic!

In 2014, Pharrell was given a star on the Hollywood Walk of Fame.

Pharrell knows that education is important. He started a benefit called From One Hand to AnOTHER. This group teaches kids about science and the arts.

Pharrell has worked with a benefit called Musicians on Call. He cheered up kids at a children's hospital.

Pharrell works with the Get Schooled Foundation. This group helps people finish high school and college.

BUZZ

Pharrell is a creative star who works in music, television, and fashion. In 2015, he was the host of an Apple radio station program. On OTHERtone, Pharrell chose what songs to play. And, he **released** a song called "Freedom." Pharrell's fans are excited to see what he does next!

Pharrell is known for his cool fashion sense. He often wears interesting hats.

GLOSSARY

award something that is given in recognition of good work or a good act.

coach someone who teaches or trains a person or a group on a certain subject or skill.

designer (dih-ZINE-ehr) someone who has ideas and works on making a plan.

Grammy Award any of the awards given each year by the National Academy of Recording Arts and Sciences. Grammy Awards honor the year's best accomplishments in music.

hip-hop a form of popular music that features rhyme, spoken words, and electronic sounds. It is similar to rap music.

inspire to bring about.

nominate to name as a possible winner.

perform to do something in front of an audience.

photograph (FOH-tuh-graf) a picture made with a camera.

pop relating to popular music.

produce to oversee the making of a movie, a play, an album, or a radio or television show. A person who does this is called a producer.

release to make available to the public.

solo a performance by a single person.

soundtrack a recording of the music featured in a movie or a television show.

WEBSITES

To learn more about Pop Biographies, visit **booklinks.abdopublishing.com**. These links are routinely monitored and updated to provide the most current information available.

INDEX